MERCURY
PLANETS IN OUR SOLAR SYSTEM
CHILDREN'S ASTRONOMY EDITION

Speedy Publishing LLC
40 E. Main St. #1156
Newark, DE 19711
www.speedypublishing.com

Copyright 2015

All Rights reserved. No part of this book may be reproduced or used in any way or form or by any means whether electronic or mechanical, this means that you cannot record or photocopy any material ideas or tips that are provided in this book

Mercury is the closest
planet to the Sun.

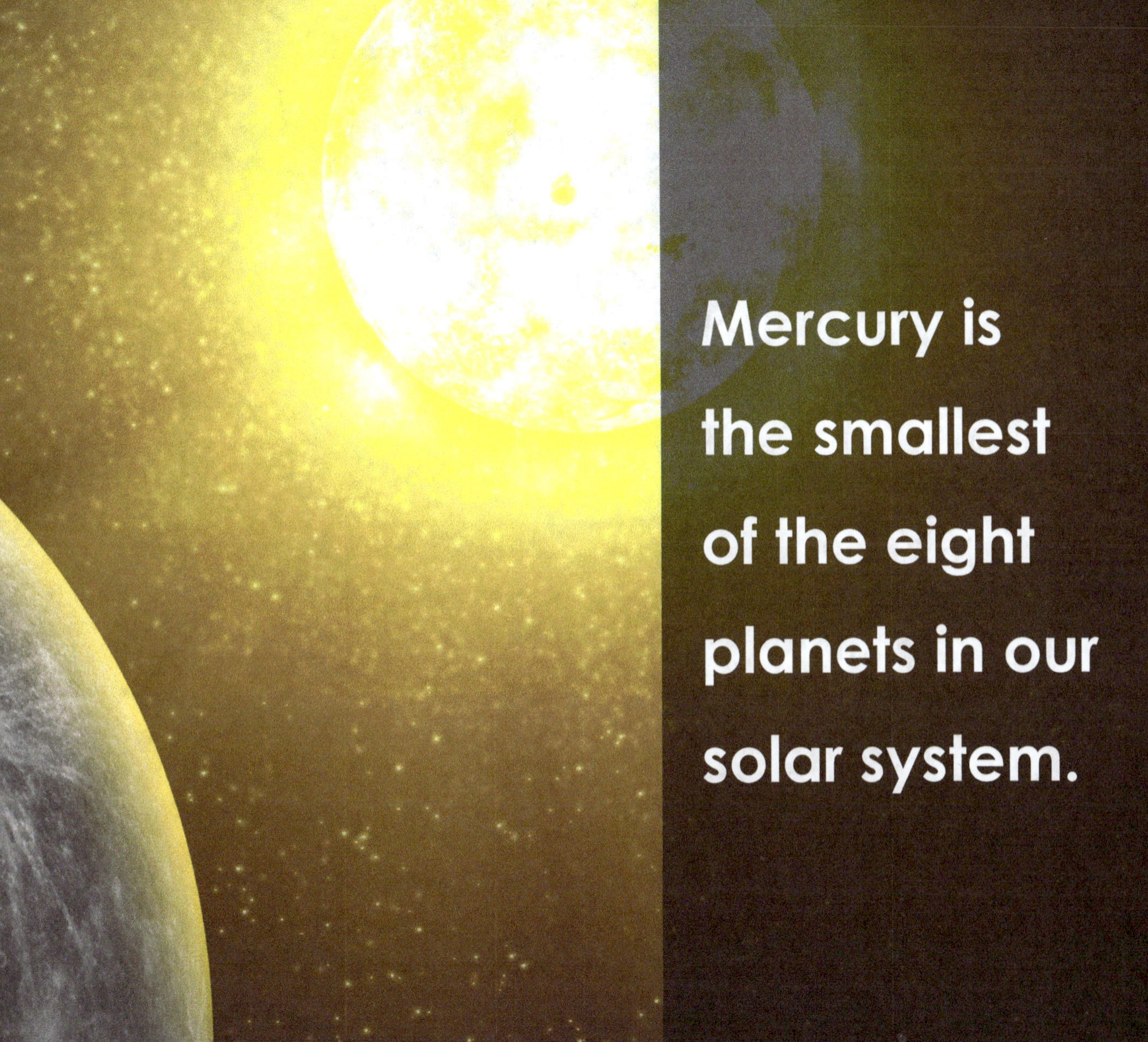

Mercury is
the smallest
of the eight
planets in our
solar system.

Mercury orbits
around the
Sun. Its orbit
lasts for only
88 days.

The daytime temperature on Mercury is reaching over 400 Degrees Celsius.

At night, the temperatures plummet, dropping to -180 Degrees Celsius.

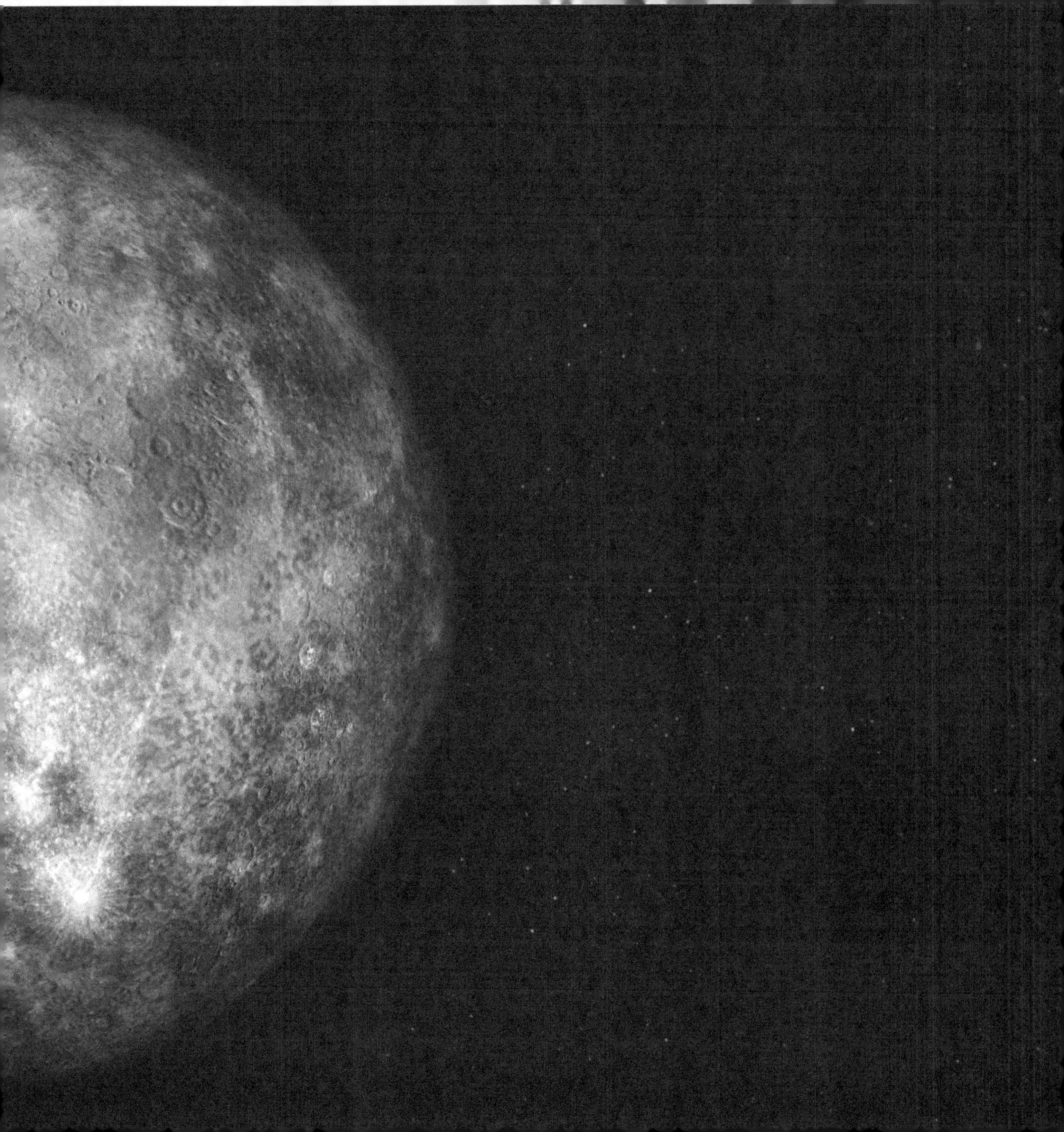

Mercury
has no
atmosphere
which means
there is no
wind or
weather to
speak of.

When Mercury orbits the Sun, it travels 36 million miles in the 88 days of the orbit.

Mercury turns
very slowly on
its axis, taking
59 days to
complete
the turn from
day to night.

Mercury has

no known

natural

satellites.

The planet
is named
after the
Roman deity
Mercury, the
messenger
to the gods.

Mercury
can appear
in Earth's
sky in the
morning or
the evening.

Mercury's core has a higher iron content than that of any other major planet in the Solar System.

Mercury was heavily bombarded by comets and asteroids during and shortly following its formation 4.6 billion years ago.

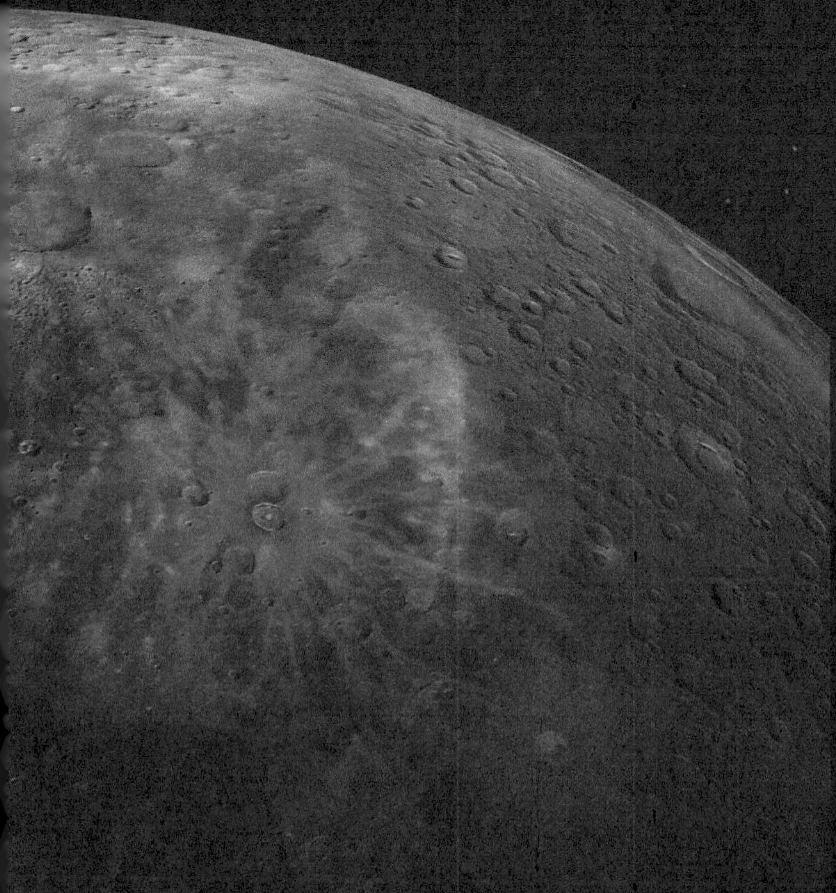

There is no
water on the
surface of
Mercury.

There is also
no air on the
surface of
Mercury.

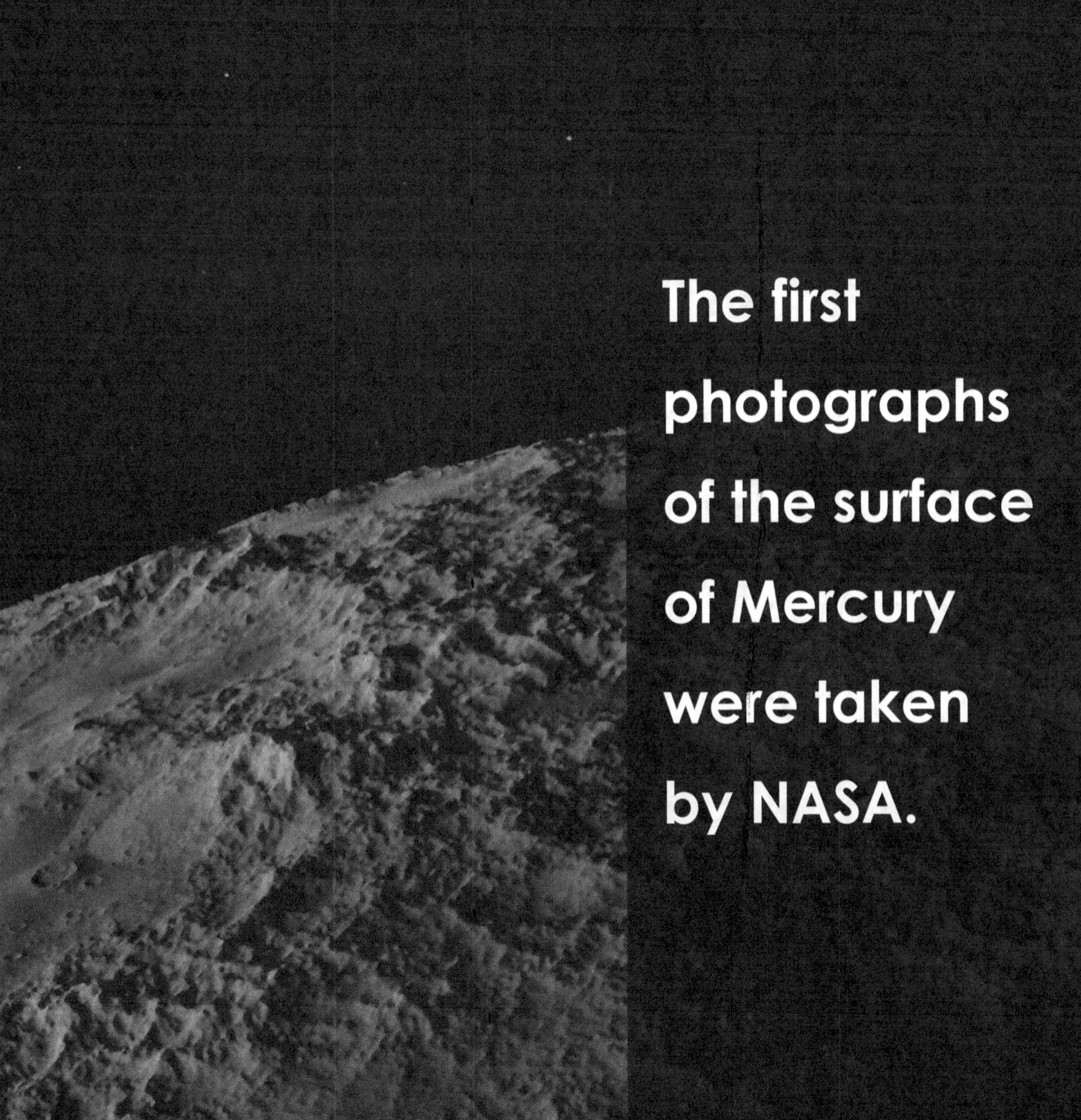
The first
photographs
of the surface
of Mercury
were taken
by NASA.

NASA's latest mission to Mercury is called Messenger. The Messenger entered Mercury's orbit in March 2011.

Mercury is one of five
planets that can be seen
without using a telescope.

Mercury

is only the

second

hottest

planet. Venus

experiences

higher

temperatures.

www.ingramcontent.com/pod-product-compliance
Lightning Source LLC
Chambersburg PA
CBHW082104130726
48003CB00009BA/3051